]
and the

MW01135958

by Alice Bullock

SUNSTONE PRESS

Copyright © 1978 by Alice Bullock. All rights reserved.

Printed and bound in the United States of America. No part of this book may be reproduced in any form or by any electronic or mechanical means including information storage and retrieval systems without permission in writing from the publisher, except by a reviewer who may quote brief passages in a review.

Sunstone books may be purchased for educational, business, or sales promotional use. For information please write: Special Markets Department, Sunstone Press, P.O. Box 2321, Santa Fe, New Mexico 87504-2321.

Library of Congress Cataloging-in-Publication Data:

Bullock, Alice, 1904–1986
    Loretto and the miraculous staircase
    1. Santa Fe, N.M. Loretto Chapel. 2. Loretto Academy.
    3. Santa Fe, N.M. —History. I. Title.
NA5235.S2686B84   978.9'56   78-18526
    ISBN: 0-913270-80-6

Published by SUNSTONE PRESS
              Post Office Box 2321
              Santa Fe, NM 87504-2321 / USA
              (505) 988-4418 / *orders only* (800) 243-5644
              FAX (505) 988-1025
              www.sunstonepress.com

LORETTO

At the downtown beginning of the Old Santa Fe Trail (once College Street) a girls' school stood for over a century on the left hand side of the thoroughfare. Loretto Academy was founded by the Sisters of Loretto in 1852 when Bishop (later Archbishop) John B. Lamy persuaded these worthy ladies that a school for females was very much needed. It was, during the many years it stood there, always a fine school, and many are the women still living in Santa Fe who can proudly boast, "I went to Loretto." It was both a boarding and day school with the best families all over the northern part of the state bringing their daughters to Loretto for their education—scholastic, musical and spiritual. The great soft-red brick buildings resounded to happy laughter, class recitations, choir and instrumental practice hours, and the rustle of the long black habits as the Sisters hurried here and there.

Lamy was pleased with the school, happy that girls were being given the opportunity to learn as well as the boys farther up the street at St. Michael's College. St. Michael's college ultimately moved and became The College of Santa Fe, but the name St. Michael's still lives on as a high school out on Siringo Road. The bishop was not happy, however, that the Sisters and girls did not have a chapel of their very own.

When Lamy felt that something was needed, whether it be schooling, a cathedral or whatever, he did something about it. He recalled the small Sainte-Chapelle in Paris. Small, yes, but a little jewel. Why not reproduce it in essence for Loretto? A young French architect was hired and plans were drawn up. Stonemasons went to work and on July 25, 1873, the walls began to reach for the sky. The Sisters measured with their eyes the progress made each day, and the young ladies, in their modest white blouses and dark skirts, watched the workmen and marveled, seeing a rose window for the first time in their young lives, and undoubtedly one or two very brash ones promised themselves to someday go to Mass in the Paris chapel that was being repeated here in the shadow of the Sangre de Cristos.

Lamy inspected the progress as often as he could, talking with the young architect, chatting with Sister

Blandina (who wrote *At the End of the Santa Fe Trail*, which is well worth reading) and often, too, with his nephew and the nephew's lovely young wife.

That lovely wife drew the attention of the young architect much too strongly. The nephew objected and undoubtedly there were many bitter quarrels. The nephew forbade the architect's calling at their home, and his wife, with a streak of independence rare in that age packed her bags and moved to The Exchange Hotel (now La Fonda). The good ladies in the Altar Society whispered this astonishing bit of news and commented, each in her own way. Did the Bishop know? They dared not ask, nor did the Church official give any public notice. The nephew, distraught at the disintegration of his marriage, sought out the architect and warned him yet again to stay away from his wife on pain of death.

The architect ignored the threat and paid with his life. Young Lamy saw him emerge from his wife's room at the hotel, drew a pistol, and shot him. This all has a bearing on the Chapel. Drawings were there and workmen could and did complete the Chapel, all except one thing. The choir loft was complete, so was the rest of the Chapel, but the plans showed no way to ascend to that choir loft. No stair, inside or out, led up. Putting in an ordinary stair would have ruined the appearance of the Chapel interior besides

severely cutting in the seating space. (One wonders what arrangements pertained in the original Sainte-Chapelle.) The architect was dead. What to do?

Carpenters and builders were called in, only to shake their heads in despair. The good Sisters of Loretto were in a quandary. When all else had failed, the Sisters determined to pray a novena to the Master Carpenter himself, St. Joseph. The gray dawn hours were the only ones not on their strenuous schedule. They rose an hour earlier and hurried to the Chapel altar, their fingers slipping over their rosaries bead by bead.

One the ninth day, Mother Superior was called back to her office. A workman wanted to see her. His burro stood patiently outside the door, loaded with carpenter's tools. The Man—no ordinary name has ever been ascribed to him—told Mother he felt he could solve the problem of the access to the choir loft. All he wanted was a couple of large water tubs and her permission. Mother Superior gave both and he quietly went to work.

Sisters, going in to the the Chapel to pray, saw the tubs with wood soaking in them, but the Man always withdrew while they said their prayers, returning to his work when the Chapel was free. Some there are who say the circular stair which stands

there today was built very quickly. Others say no, it took quite a little time. But the stair did grow, rising solidly in a double helix without support of any kind and without a nail or screw. The floor space used was minimal and the stair adds to, rather than detracts from, the beauty of the Chapel.

The Sisters were overjoyed and planned a fine dinner to honor the Carpenter. Only he could not be found. No one seemed to know him, where he lived, nothing. Lumberyards were checked, but they had no bill for the Sisters of Loretto. They had not sold him the wood. Knowledgeable men went in and inspected the stair and none knew what kind of wood had been used, certainly nothing indigenous to this area. Advertisements for the Carpenter were run in the *New Mexican* and brought no response.

"Surely," said the devout, "it was St. Joseph himself who built the stair."

Whether it was built miraculously or by a skilled craftsman, not one cent was ever paid anyone for the stair. Nor is it known whether the bannister was put on then or added later. Certainly no repairs have been made or needed through the years save a small patching job on the plaster backing. That was done because visitors had picked out a minor hole, carrying away small fragments of the plaster as souvenirs, possibly

feeling that they were bits of a holy relic.

When the Loretto site was sold, a clause in the deed provided that the chapel should be kept intact. During the tearing down of the school buildings a fire broke out on the upper floor of one building. The fire sirens shrilled and all over Santa Fe there was consternation was word passed from one to another, "Fire at Loretto!" Old wood flared hotly, and wind fanned the blaze. No one cared about the school building—but would the fire spread to the Chapel? The fire fighters worked rapidly, their figures showing through swirling smoke, only to disappear again as wind caught and eddied around them and the building. On the streets people unashamedly stopped and their lips moved in prayer. Loretto Chapel is loved by all denominations and creeds as a thing of beauty. When the last flame was extinguished the Chapel stood unharmed. The vagrant winds blew the hot breath of the fire away from the Chapel.

With the demolition of the old school building completed, Loretto Inn was erected with the Pueblo architecture fitting in completely right for the ancient city of the Holy Faith. The Inn is lovely, inside and out. Girls who were once students at the school put on their prettiest gowns to attend a banquet on the site where once they struggled with algebra or wrote themes. Visitors from all over the country, as

well as abroad, relax in the quiet atmosphere where the Sisters of Loretto conducted a school.

Once in a while, the organ in the Chapel will swell to the strains of the wedding march, for a small wedding is held here to be treasured in memory.

The black-robed Sisters make no claims for "La Escalera Famosa." Visitors are charged a small fee, only enough to maintain the Chapel, to keep it clean and lovely. The stair stands in graceful splendor, an inspiration for all. Visitors are not ordinarily allowed to climb it because there is no other egress in case of a fire. This writer has climbed it by special permission to photograph it. There is a very slight vibration as one ascends and descends rather as though the stair were a living, breathing thing.

Whether it was the work of St. Joseph or an inspired man, no visit to Santa Fe is complete that misses The Miraculous Stair—or to translate the Spanish—the Famous Stair.

Everything, including a city, is more fun when you know more about it. Santa Fe, called "The City Different," is fascinating and the following books—all published by Sunstone Press—could increase your enjoyment.

CHRISTMAS IN OLD SANTA FE
by Pedro Ribera Ortega

LA CONQUISTADORA, THE STORY OF A FAMOUS
RELIGIOUS STATUE by Fray Angelico Chavez

SAINT FRANCIS MURALS, THE STORY OF THE
MURALS IN THE SAINT FRANCIS AUDITORIUM
AND THE ARTIST WHO PAINTED THEM
by Carl Sheppard

SANTA FE THEN AND NOW
by Sheila Morand

YESTERDAY IN SANTA FE
by Marc Simmons

You can get these books in most bookstores or order them directly.

Write Sunstone Press at Box 2321, Santa Fe, NM 87504-2321;

Or visit the Sunstone Press web site at
www.sunstonepress.com.

CPSIA information can be obtained
at www.ICGtesting.com
Printed in the USA
BVOW03s0938070617

486285BV00001B/113/P

9 780913 270806